Making, Playing & Composing

on the

10 Stringed Lyre-Harp

By
Abbot David Michael, MEd, MS, DD, ThD
Priory of Jerusalem

All Copyrights Protected
ISBN# 978-0692268537
Edition 1.0 (proof edition)
update: 2 August 2014

**Taught as a Class at the Campbell Folk School, NC.
info@folkschool.org, 1-800-FOLK-SCH**

Glentivar Village Press
PO Bx 301, Hartsel, CO 80449
info@glentivar.org

Prologue

There is a revival of the ancient Lyre now returning into the arms of those who live for romance and enlightenment. With the simple to play lyre, one can sing the songs of the ancients in capturing the free sounds of nature, love, passion and in worship to God and in telling the stories of heroes.

In this book, I have attempted to make the building of the lyre harp as simple as possible. I have tried to explain the tuning of the instrument sound wood during construction. Very few books reveal the 'secret' of how to make an instrument sing in resonance with every note that is played. This is normally a trade secret and only divulged to the most promising of students by the master Luthier. My teacher George Gilmore, a celebrated student of Andre' Segovia would not tell me directly. He had me discover this for myself and later I had it confirmed from an old German violin maker.

Not only are you going to learn how to make a lyre harp, you will learn how to tune it, play it in its diatonic scale of A major and transpose songs as needed. That is not all. You will even learn how to compose new songs on the lyre using a simple composing method that dates back to era of King David in circa 1000 BCE.

In the writing of this book, I would like to thank the harp making class I taught at the Campbell Folk School in North Carolina. Most of the pictures in this book are from that class and made this book possible.

I received much good advice about what in the draft of this booked worked and what did not work. Many thanks... you were a great class! David

Contents

1. History 4
2. Types of Lyres 10
3. Tools 11
4. Choosing Wood 13
5. Acoustical Theory 16
6. Design 20
7. Making the Frame 22
8. Top and Back 26
9. Finishing 31
10. Hardware 34
11. Ornamentation 38
12. Electrics 39
13. Tuning 40
14. Playing 43
15. Transposing 45
16. Songs 48
17. Composing 58
18. Phrase Cards 62
19. Harp Pattern 64
20. Kits & Bio 65

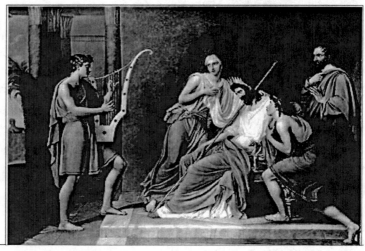

The picture to the right is David playing the lyre harp for King Saul to drive away the evil spirits from him. Did it work? Yes... for a while it seems. But finally David had to run for his life to escape the jealousy of King Saul who wanted to kill him. In the end, David became King and his favorite instrument, the Lyre was preserved for us today.

1. History of the Lyre

Ancient Origins

The origin of the Lyre type harp predates the triangular harp by perhaps a thousands of years. It dates back to the Sumerians in circa 4000 BCE who were the first advanced civilization noted in history where music in a more refined form was used to bring comfort, tell stories, provide the beat for the dance and to worship and pray to the gods.

From the Sumerians, it migrated to what became Israel with Abraham of the Bible who left Ur of the Chaldees circa 2700 BCE. It found its way among the proto-Babylonians under its founding master, King Nimrod. These two dominant civilizations in the fertile crescent became rivals at war yet both had music, song and the lyre instrument as core to their cultures.

It is also evident in history that it came again to Babylon in the time of King Nebuchadnezzar with the arrival of the Hebrew prophet Daniel and thousands of Israelites when they were overcome in battle. All of the nobles of Israel were exiled into slavery and carried off to Babylon with their lyres and harps. They were so sad

due to this enslavement, they vowed not to play the lyre and harp again until they returned to Israel. In protest, they hung their instruments in the willow trees in Babylon in circa 720 BCE. (Psalm 137).

Israel Revival

Earlier during the time of King David in about 1000 BCE, there was a renaissance of music, architecture and the arts. The lyre being improved upon settling with a 10 stringed version called the Kinnor was then used by the priests in the worship of YHWH in the Tabernacle.

There is now compelling

evidence that the Temple music under Solomon used a diatonic scale (7 notes to the next octave) and this was passed on to future generations and civilizations. Different songs of the bible were sung in different modes that were later codified by the Greeks with the new scales or keys starting on different notes of the 7 note diatonic scale.

The Greeks took one diatonic key scale and started from the different notes in the scale to change the key to different tunings.

The basic lyre harp design that was common in King David's day was kept intact until 132 AD when it was imprinted on a Hebrew coin during the Bar Kochba Rebellion. It is this coin (above and right) from which the basic design dimensions originate for the lyre harp lyre as it exists today.

Egypt

The Hebrews now called the Israelites went to Egypt under a friendly pharaoh when a severe drought occurred in Israel. Sadly as time ran its course, the later Ramses Pharaohs (19th dynasty) became afraid at their prolific expansion of numbers and they were enslaved to build pyramids and other sacred buildings. In the below painting in Egypt, we see the Semites (Israel?) while in slavery in Egypt about the time of Moses holding and playing a lyre harp while they are marching in procession.

There is evidence in Egyptian history that the Pharaoh Aye (18th dynasty) was none other than Ephraim, the son of Joseph, the son of Jacob who was called Israel. He married the daughter of a Pharaoh and thus became a Pharaoh since the Egyptian royal line was carried through the female royals. This dynasty of Hebrew Pharaohs were known as the 'Shepherd Kings' and they ruled Egypt for a short time in turning Egypt to worshiping the one God.

This forced conversion to one god was short lived as the 18th dynasty were usurped with many Hebrew Israelites being driven from the land of Egypt. It is known that the lyre was played all through this period evident in the pictographs found in the many architectural wonders of Egypt.

Troy

The Hebrews who did not leave Egypt later became enslaved under the Ramses pharaohs but were later freed by Moses as per biblical history. The ones who left in an earlier migration are believed by some scholars to have founded the city of Troy and became the famous Trojans.

Troy became another revival center for the arts and music with many love songs being written from all over Greece to the beautiful Queen Helen of Troy . When they were overcome in circa 1188 BCE, this same Hebrew stock were thought to have migrated to the British Isles and lived among the Celts and Picts in Ireland near Tara.

In about 1000 BCE, the legendary king Ollav Folla seemed to have Hebrew connections and lived during the same time as King David in Israel . Ollav was accredited with creating the laws of Ireland that mirror closely the Levitical laws of the Hebrews that later became known as the Brechan laws in Ireland. This suggests a possible communication between Israel and Ireland during this time in history.

They took with them the lyre that had gone through many cultural revisions and forms but still retained the horns at the top, a space for the left had to play through from the back and a sound box with the strings strung over the front of the instrument.

Ireland and Scotland

In circa 500 BCE, Jeremiah the Prophet of Israel migrated with a company of Israelites and the daughters of King Zedekiah to the far West. Israel had succumb in war tot he King of Babylon where King Zedekiah and his royal sons were captured and brought brought to Babylon where they were first blinded and then killed.

Jeremiah being the great-grandfather of King Zedekiah's royal children took the two remaining daughters and left in what is today France and the other to Ireland out of the reach of Egypt, Greece and Babylon. The royal daughter of the line of King David named Tamar Telphi was then married to Eochaid I (Heremon) in about500 BCE , who was the High King of Ireland. From this union, the High Kings of Ireland became directly descended from the royal line of King David as were the later early Scottish Kings. It is thought by some researchers that the original harps of King David are still buried in the tomb of Jeremiah near Tara, Ireland that exists there today. This tomb has never been allowed to be excavated.

The Celts of Ireland then called the Scotti by the 4th century AD sailed across the Irish channel and founded a country in what is now Argyle, Scotland and brought with them the lyre. King Aedan of the royal line of the High Kings of Ireland was crowned by the prophet St. Columba (Colum Cille) of Iona who also was also a descendent of the High Kings of Ireland and of the Royal line of King David.

King Aedan mac Gabran was coronated on the Stone of Scone also known as the Stone of Destiny. The historic Stone of Destiny is the sacred Israelite stone brought to Ireland by Jeremiah. This stone was the same stone that Jacobs slept upon as he saw the angels asending and descending from heaven and became the sacred coronaiton stone for the line of King David upoin the earth. It was this very stone upon which King David was crowned in Israel by the prophet Samuel. It was then that Jacob's name was changed from Jacob to Israel by YHWH.

King Aedan according to ancient Culdee history became the King of Dal Riada which is where Camelot was built located somewhere between Glasgow and Edinburgh in Scotland. Aedan became the father of the famous King Arthur although there is no record Arthur was any more than a crowned prince but he did serve with his father as perhaps a Co-Regent and General in fighting against the Picts and the invading Anglo-Saxons (English).

Yes... earliest records place Camelot in Scotland somewhere between Glasgow and Edinburgh and not in Wales or England. It was there that the lyre first found its new home in Scotland. It may have been there in the castle of Camelot that the lyre was first played to the dance and to the song as the ladies of the court dressed to impress Prince Arthur's Knights of the Round Table.

Greece and Rome

From the various locations in Mesopotamia and Egypt, the Lyre migrated to Greece possibly through the Hittites or the early Trojans and became a favored instrument by the Grecians for their musical dramas.

With the rule of Greek culture expanding rapidly under Alexander the Great (356-323 BCE), the lyre migrated over most of the known world and was adopted by emerging Rome in Italy as a favored Instrument. It is noted in history that the Roman Emperor Nero played the lyre as Rome was burning to the ground. We do not know if he was playing a sad song or a happy song at this historic event.

Figure 1 after fol. 30b, Vespasian Psalter

Sutton Hoo Lyre

Back in Britannia, the primary evidence of the lyre being used in Britannia is the Sutton Hoo Lyre which is really a later Anglo-Celtic version of the ancient Hebrew lyre. By the 6th century AD, this version of the lyre had a rounded off top rather then the more traditional 'horns' that were common among earlier BCE lyres.

The 6 strings of this lyre suggests a pentatonic tuning with the root tone reoccurring as an octave higher tone. Its tuning would be Do' Re' Mi' – So' La' – Do' as its So-Feg scale or if using interval numbers it would be: 1 , 2, 3 – 5, 6 – 8.

However, many songs of the period only go from Do to La in their scale so this may also have been tuned to a diatonic scale with limited range for a single voice to sing the same notes as those played.

What is clever about the pentatonic scale is you can play any two strings a 3rd or more apart and they are

harmonic. This means using this scale always creates a pleasant sounding chord. This enables first time players to be very innovative in song writing and in singing a new song.

Many of the more traditional folk songs of the Celts, Hebrews and other ancient civilizations are written in the Pentatonic scale. However, for the temple music tuning, we find that the diatonic or full do, re, mi scales was used. Therefore for the lyre harps in this instructional, we will go with the diatonic A major tuning as this is easier to learn for the western sense of musicality.

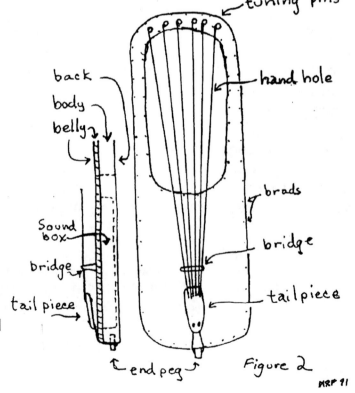

Figure 2

MRP 11

New World

With the migration of the Irish, Scots and Welsh to the new world, especially during the 1850's Irish potato famine, the Hebrew-Celtic lyre was brought to

America and became the lyre harp made today. It has regained its 'horns' as per the ancient lyres of the past to give it a more historic look. The Lyre is tuned to a diatonic scale of A Major starting on the root 1-do, 2-re, 3-mi, 4-fa, 5-so, 6-la, 7-ti, 1-do, 2-re and 3-mi.

The Lyre is most commonly found where large numbers of Celts (Scots, Irish and Welsh) first got off the boat and lived in the mountains. We find remnant oral history of the lyre being played among the mountain folk of the Adirondacks, the Ozarks, the Appellation mountains and even the Rockies.

Not wanting such a historic instrument to disappear from use, David of Battleharp.com now makes these available as a completed instrument ready to play or as a kit that may be purchased and built by most anyone with just a few hand tools.

Many of the lyres made today by David have wood-burned art embossed into there tops and backs. It was once said that a warrior was not a warrior among the Celts unless he or she had a harp, a sword and was granted the right to carry the crest

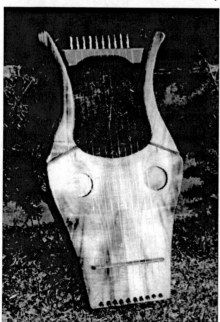

of their clan. On the harps of old among the Celts were often found symbols of the owners rank and clan. You too can now have and play a historic Lyre that dates back 6000 years as the first instrument ever made and played in civilized society. You may go to the last page of this book for more information on how to order a Mountain Lyre or a Mountain Lyre Kit.

To the left is a concert version of the Kinnor harp made of Hawaiian Koa which is a member of the Acacia wood family. This design was the first harp made in modern times by Abbot David of his design that is based upon the archeological evidence of harp design dating from 132 CE. It is believed to be the actual design of the 10 stringed harps of David of 1000 years earlier.

2. Types of Lyres

As already mentioned, there are many different designs of the lyre that were produced over the last 5000-6000 years. Here are some designs in pictures to show the variation in lyre design over the centuries found in different cultures.

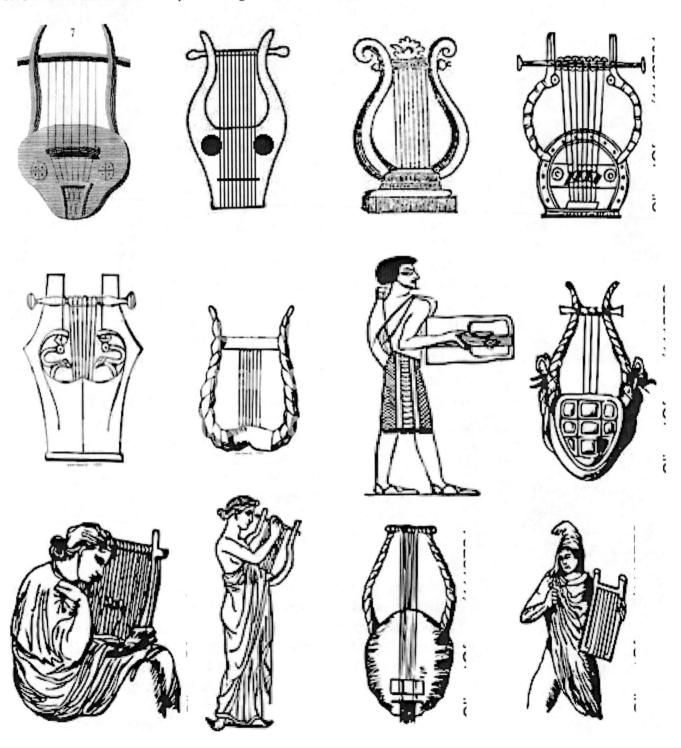

3. Tools

Hand Tools

The early lyres were of course made completely by hand with the tools then available to the local Woodsmith (Luthier).

These tools have not changed much over the last 4000 years up to the beginning of the Industrial Revolution. This Revolution hit the West with the invention of massive externally powered machines that could do the work of many men very quickly.

However, you will still see hand driven machines reminiscent of the middle ages emerge during the Industrial Revolution and even still used today that are either crank or treadle driven.

Modern Hand Tools

It does not take very many hand tools to make a lyre once you have gotten past the tree felling and splitting of the wood into usable board sizes. I have made harps with only a jack plane, coping saw, wood rasp, scraper and hand drill. This was a very slow process but rewarding to know how little is really needed to make a harp. If one totally relies on the purchase of expensive power tools before making a harp, you are preventing yourself from engaging in the process of forming the wood with honor and respect for creation. I have spent many years in very loud wood shops with massive wood working machines and realized as I got older how little contact I really had with the wood.

I would minimally recommend the following tools that all can easily fit into a small leather or canvas carry bag.

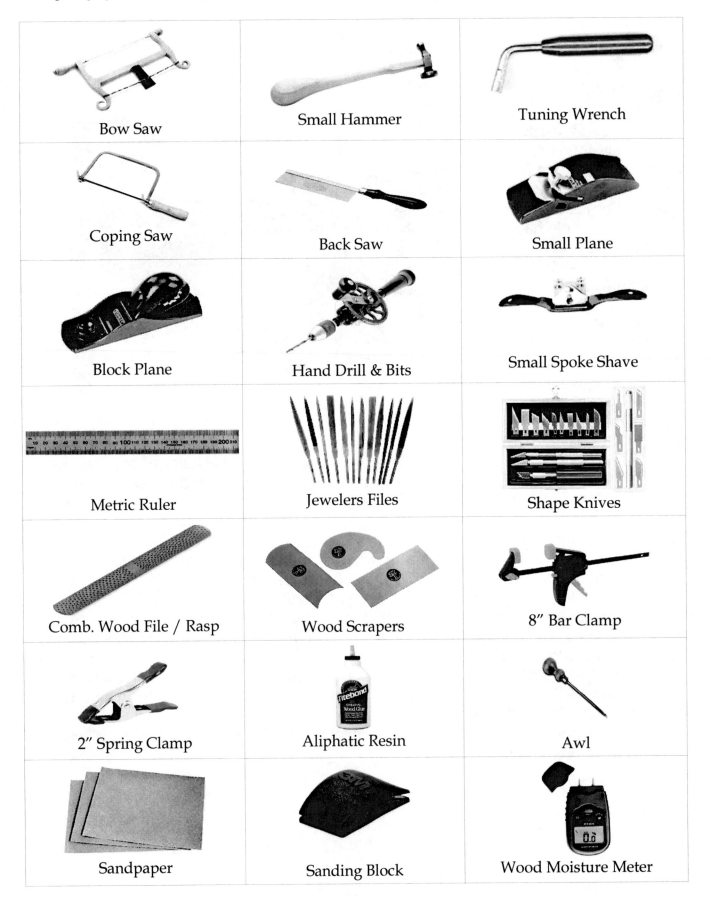

Bow Saw	Small Hammer	Tuning Wrench
Coping Saw	Back Saw	Small Plane
Block Plane	Hand Drill & Bits	Small Spoke Shave
Metric Ruler	Jewelers Files	Shape Knives
Comb. Wood File / Rasp	Wood Scrapers	8" Bar Clamp
2" Spring Clamp	Aliphatic Resin	Awl
Sandpaper	Sanding Block	Wood Moisture Meter

4. Choosing Wood

Instrument Wood

The art and science of finding the best wood for instruments is often considered a trade secret by luthiers around the world. Their source of wood is seldom revealed – especially if they harvest it themselves. It was common for the Masters of the trade to store up good instrument wood a whole generation before it was needed - over 20 years. It was then used by their sons who passed on the trade or to their sons as esteemed apprentices as they stored up wood for the next generation.

In modern times, wood is quick dried and seasoned by various methods normally using heat and is promised by commercial suppliers to be great for instruments. The fact is to heat up wood is to cause the cells in the woos to expand due to the moisture in the cells going to near steam and this presses against the cellular walls and leads to cellular breakage that destroys the potential of sound resonance and greatly weakens the wood. You cannot tell this has happened by looking at the wood with your eyes but you can by microscope. The alternative is to dry the wood over a very long period with temperatures far under 212 degrees so as to preserve the cellular structure of the wood. When dried, the moisture content should be under 8% and the inner wood stresses due to drying stabilized.

All 'great' instrument makers will only used seasoned wood that has been in a cool dry place for over 20 years. The wood is normally stored in a area where the wood was harvested. Slow growth wood especially needed for sound wood normally grows in dryer colder climates. The least stress you can put upon the wood as it dries the better.

Quarter Sawn Wood

The top and back were usually split from softer wood from a short log. The same technique used today in splitting roof shakes from cedar with a froe can also split straight grain tone wood. The top and back are cut from the outside rim of the log to the center or quarter sawn (see right). This is so the run of the grain would be vertical to the flat or thin part of the sound board for greatest strength and resonance. This is called quarter sawing or splitting the wood.

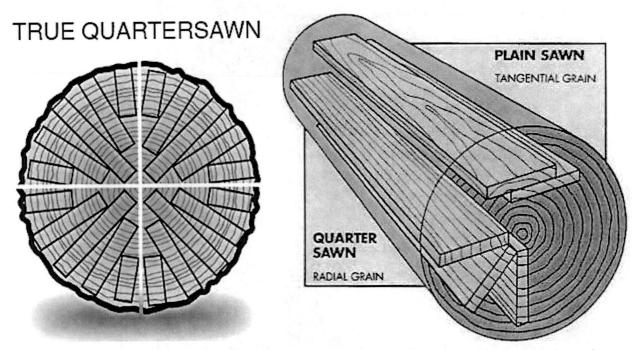

TRUE QUARTERSAWN

PLAIN SAWN
TANGENTIAL GRAIN

QUARTER SAWN

RADIAL GRAIN

The harder ring grain of the wood chosen should be properly spaced - about 1/16" to 1/8" apart. The softer wood between the harder grain allows the harder grain to vibrate freely like resonating 'reeds' with the softer grain giving way to let this happen.

Finding Tone Wood

I have used many different kinds of tone wood for sound boards. Some very inexpensive woods suitable for tone wood can be found at your local hardware store. Shakes and shingles are normally quarter split and then sawn. A good sized shake or shingle if long enough for your design can become an excellent sound board. In a square of shakes, you will often find two such shingles close together split from the same log that are book matched.

I also have used inexpensive 5/8" thick red cedar fencing for sound wood. You just have to go through the stack to find boards that are accidentally quarter sawn and clear of knots. I go through 100 boards 6' by 5.5" wide to find perhaps one board. If you cut the board in half with a band saw or bow saw with guides, you get two pieces that are book matched and great for soundboards.

This wood is usually very wet and must be dried for months before using it for tone wood. A wood moisture meter is good to have to test your wood before using it in an instrument with a moisture reading under 8%. Wet wood if used on an instrument will dry over time, shrink then split and ruin the instrument.

Before cutting the shape of the sound boards (top and back) you will need to glue your frame together so you know the size of the cuts.

Harvesting Wood

To embark on making a lyre begins with choosing the best tree and getting the wood you want from the tree and then storing it for 20 years. If you do not want to wait that long, find wood that has been dead for 20 years and protected from the weather in a cool dry place. For lower cost instruments, reasonable sound wood can be cut thin (close to final thickness) and then stored in a dry place for 6 months and used without concern for splitting and undue internal stresses.

The historic method of harvesting a large tree employed a tree saw or felling ax. Then the wood was split with wedges and hammers to get boards. It was split so the grain would run completely parallel with the length of the wood to keep it it the strongest possible.

The planing of the wood after splitting was done initially with an adze, then wooden block planes and finished up with scrapers. The making of the holes for the tuning keys was normally done by a hand drill and bit. If this was not available, the hole could be made with a hot small metal poker and then reamed out to fit the wooden tuning key.

If you needed a curved piece for your instrument, you would either find a curved branch about the right size or steam a straight piece to get it to bend. Still, the grain would remain parallel with the length of the wood even if bent which is very important since some instruments can have tons or pressure on them from the tension of of the strings.

5. Acoustical Theory

The theory of sound occurring in an instrument to make music for the lyre is very complex. As an example, it has been the attempt of science to find out how the Stradivarius violin makes its beautiful sound acoustically and then to duplicate it to sell. The problem is there are so many variable factors that is makes it very difficult if not impossible to achieve in mass production.

Sound Wood

What is most difficult to standardize is the wood used in an instrument. It is now believed that the wood used by Stradivarius was taken from a bog where it was suspended for perhaps hundreds of years and absorbed natural chemicals from the bog and this changed the nature of its wood. If you change the chemical nature of the wood, you change the sound or harmonic overtones of the wood when it resonates. This one factor cannot be duplicated.

However, we can take good resonating wood and cut and hon it to a dimension that will provide the best sound possible for its characteristics. We can design the resonating box such that is will sing with a dominate tone or pitch when tapped. The size of the sound hole will also change the sound of the resonating box with a larger hole giving way to lower tones and a smaller hole giving way to higher tones in the harmonic overtone series.

Compression Waves Make Sound

Sound is a compression wave and it occurs when an object has a rapid back and forth movement in the air that compresses and decompresses the air molecules in a consistent cycle or 'times per second'. For us to hear it, the back and forth movement has to be normally no less than 20 cycles per second up to about 20,000 cycle per second. Our larynx vibrates back and forth at certain speeds and this is how the sound of our voice is made for talking and singing.

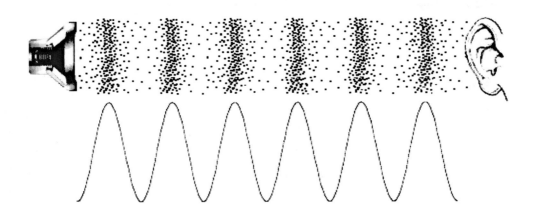

When this cycle of high and low air pressure hits our ears, the pressure wave is funneled to our ear drum that vibrates with the frequency of the sound. It is then converted to intelligible 'sound' by our brains as a specific frequency or many frequencies. If you played in instrument in a complete vacuum, it would produce no sound waves at all since there are no air molecules to compress and decompress to carry the sound waves through the vacuum.

All Note / Tone Resonance

Considering we will want our instrument to vibrate equally and freely when all of the potential strings / notes / tones are played, we must design acoustically some part of our instrument that will resonate easily with all of the tones we will be playing. We also need to make sure the lower notes we will play that vibrate slowly will have some part of the instrument that is loose or relaxed enough to vibrate more slowly to support these lower tones.

Keep in mind that longer, fatter (more mass) and looser strings make a lower tone. This is also true in an instrument. There has to be parts of the instrument that are looser and longer to allow for low tone resonance. In wood, it is less mass or thinner wood that is 'looser' and is more easily vibrated for lower tones. So, we want longer lengths of wood, thinner wood and a softer wood which allows for the lower tones to be strongly resonated and heard while assuring we retain the strength of the wood to survive the 'tearing apart' pressure of the strings.

The parts of the instrument that can be considered separate vibrating areas include the top, the back and the size of the sound box as balanced with the size of the sound hole. These three variables in combination with a good resonating wood for the instrument will make the instrument produce the best possible sound with the materials available. To discover the best resonating tones for our instrument, we need to consult the overtone series to see how nature works with sound.

Overtone Series

The overtone series is a process where the long vibration of a fundamental tone is naturally divided into smaller tones. If you think of sound as sound waves, you get the following natural subsections from one tone played.

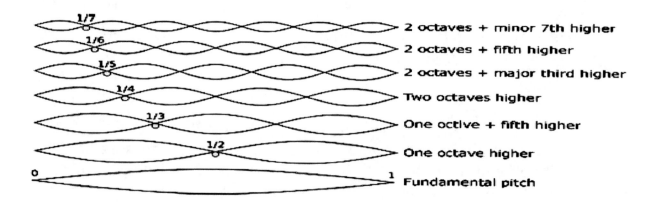

1/7 — 2 octaves + minor 7th higher
1/6 — 2 octaves + fifth higher
1/5 — 2 octaves + major third higher
1/4 — Two octaves higher
1/3 — One octive + fifth higher
1/2 — One octave higher
0 — 1 Fundamental pitch

From the divisions of the overtone series seen n the chart above, we can now translate these into notes and their specific sequence of intervals as follows using the tone of low C as the fundamental tone.

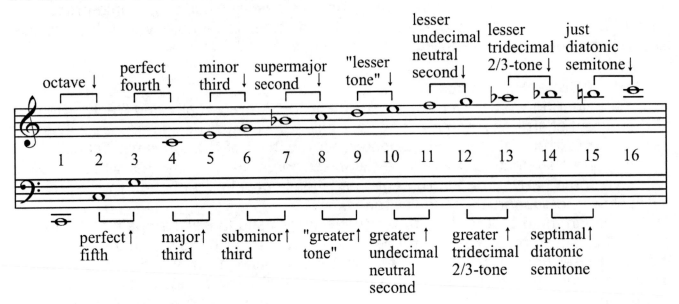

Scale of the Lyre

The key is to achieving this goal is to first analyze the natural overtone series and let these fundamental notes become your guide for designing a lyre. Since our lyre is to be designed for the key of 'A', we will begin this process by analyzing the overtone series for the note of the diatonic scale of 'A' Major provided below.

A major scale

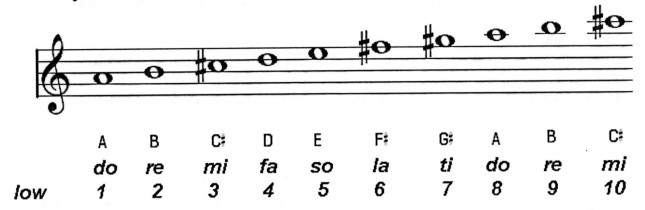

	A	B	C♯	D	E	F♯	G♯	A	B	C♯
	do	re	mi	fa	so	la	ti	do	re	mi
low	1	2	3	4	5	6	7	8	9	10

Resonance in the Lyre

Since 'A' resonates strongly with the first overtone note of 'A' an octave higher then 'E' which is a perfect 5th and then it resonates with the note of 'C#' which is a Major 3rd and then follows to the next harmonic as a Minor 3rd which when played becomes A minor which also is a very comfortable sound to our ears.

This is why the Major triad of A-C#-E is so comfortable to listen to followed by the Minor triad of A-C-E as also comfortable because both occur early on and naturally in the harmonic overtone series when you hear the single note or tone of 'A' played which is 440 cycles per second in equal temperament tuning.

We still need the notes of F#, G#, D and B to have some part of the instrument to resonate with our A major scale. Let's experiment and take the 2nd above A which is B and discover its overtone series. B when played provides for B, D and F# in its primary overtone series. We are still missing the part of the instrument that will resonate for G# which is OK for the pentatonic scale but not good if the instrument is tuned to a diatonic scale of 'A' Major.

Since the 5th is the strongest overtone, lets now try the 5th of A for this. This would be E, G# and B in the series. If we choose this, we have gained G# but now lost the D resonance. Lets try the 4th above A. D, F# and A would then be sounded. Now we are again missing the 'G#' resonance again.

Three-Part Tuning

To resolve this incomplete list of tones for a diatonic scale that needs resonance, we should remember we have three parts of our instrument that can be tuned. Lets use 'A' as the fundamental tone with the 4th (D) and the 5th (E) to capture all of the needed resonate tones.

I:	A = A, C# and E	Sound Box
IV:	D = D, F# and A	Top Soundboard
V:	E = E, G# and B	Back Soundboard

Having the instrument which now provides resonance for: A – B – C# - D – E – F# - G# - A, we have solved the problem. With this solution, we have all of the notes in both the pentatonic and the diatonic scale of A Major corresponding with some part of the instrument that will resonate when any one of the strings are played. I will show later in this book how to tune the, 1) sound box, the 2) top soundboard and the, 3) back of the lyre to one of these three tones being A, D and E.

6. Design

Discovering Tone Change

Now that we have reviewed acoustical theory and the tones we want to apply to our lyre design with the optimum tuning of the sound box, top and back, we can now design the lyre. The design could involve changing the overall size of the instrument to gain the desired box resonance and there are ways to do this mathematically but it is rather complex. More likely we will just change the thickness of the top, the back and the size of the sound hole during construction.

The challenge that is largely overcome by trial and error is that a piece of tone wood floating free and tapped will have one tone but when you glue the wood onto the instrument, the natural resonant tone will be much higher since you have now restricted the wood from freely vibrating at lower tones by gluing it to the sides.

One way to discover the right thickness and brace design for the tone wood is to build a bunch of instruments all with different sized sound boxes and then choose the best sounding one and model this assuming you have the same wood to work with each time. If you can't get all of the same wood from the same tree, what do you do?

Rule of Thumb – a 5th

One of the secrets developed in violin making to resolve this without building a bunch of instruments is to assume the back and top will increase in pitch by about a major 5th when glued to the sides. This estimate was originally determined by building a bunch of violins and then playing them all and then choosing the best one while documenting very specifically how it was designed and built. This rule of thumb seems to work in making lyres, guitars, cigar box instruments and other instruments as well....well.... most of the time. We will get more into this in the tuning of the wood section in chapter 6.

Modification after Gluing

When a larger instrument is constructed, it is common for the maker to go in through the sound hole and shave down the bracing to lower the tap tone pitch of both the back and the top in tuning the instrument. If there is no internal bracing such as with the lyre, then the top and back tones can only be lowered by reducing some of the wood from the surface of the top and back as needed until you hear the right tone. The sound box is tuned lower by slightly increasing the size of the sound hole.

If the sound hole gets too big, it will not let the instrument resonate as all the sound will go immediately out of the hole and not bounce around in the instrument to resonate the other parts of the instrument. Many makers will make the sound hole smaller than what they expect it to be when done so they can then tune the box accordingly by slightly increasing its size after the instrument is made.

7. Making the Frame

Purpose of the Frame

The frame is the first part of the instrument to cut out and put together. To save hard wood, there is just one small pattern that is used twice in making two pieces that are then glued together to make the frame of the harp. Because the frame is in two parts, it is possible to add colorful wood strips or purfling to the glue joints to provide eye-catching ornamentation to the instrument.

The frame is the structural member of the instrument and although it does provide some resonance, its primary function is to hold the instrument together under the tension of the strings. For the lyre, there are only three points where it is glued and held together. It is glued at the base of the instrument, then at the lower part of the hand hole and finally where the strings are attached to the tuning keys as the top bridge of the instrument. The most important joint is the top bridge joint since the tuning keys are attached there and there is no top or back to provide additional reinforcement.

Cutting the Frame

The frame of the instrument holds the instrument together in the making of a lyre. Some instruments do not have full instrument frames but are more uni-body in their design such as guitars, violins and other common instruments. The lyre does have a complete frame that holds the instrument together with the top and back not being under pressure except for the floating bridge to transfer the sound of the strings to the instrument for the amplification of sound.

Historically the cutting out the frame from prepared full 1" boards was often done with a bow saw or a coping saw but today usually is cut with a power band saw or good jig saw as illustrated.

Even the sound hole can be cut with a coping saw with both of these saws allowing for easily cutting tight curves in wood. For real fine work such as making a Rosette for the sound hole, a jewelers saw is used with a very fine blade abut the width is a fine wire.

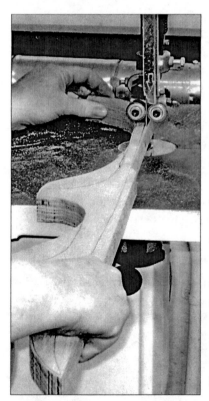

Drawing the Pattern

The pattern can be transferred to a piece of wood in such a way to conserve wood. If you flip over the pattern and trace it onto the wood upside down, you can nest in the parts in order to use less wood that otherwise. Go to the back of this book for the pattern from which to draw a template for your frame.

Once the pattern is drawn and to begin cutting, use a thin band saw blade (about 1/4") if tight curves are needed to be cut in your frame. After cutting out the frame in the rough from a template made from the plans in the back of this book, it is good to sand all of the inside cut surfaces so they are uniform in shape and finish to 120 grit before gluing. A drum reciprocating sander is the most efficient power tool for this step. A drum sander on a drill can also be used. If hand tools are used, take a curved wood rasp and file to clean up the rough cuts then sand by hand.

Preparing the Joints

Once cut out in the rough and sanded, put them together to see how the three glue joints line up. If they are not perfectly aligned in touching across the whole glue joint for all three joints, cut and sand as needed to assure a tight joint. Be very careful not to round off the corners of the joints as this will leave gaps and make the joint weak. If using a smaller belt sander like a 4" by 36" sander, rig a board out from the sander the same height as the sander bed on which to place the end of the side to assure the sanding is even across all three joints.

The best way is to hand sand all three joints at the same time is by using a long board with 80-120 grit sandpaper glued to it. Or, you could use a large belt sander. If hand sanding, add to this sanding board a 90 degree upright board on one side to assure you do not tilt the frame sides and round off the joint edges. Sand both pieces until they fit perfectly.

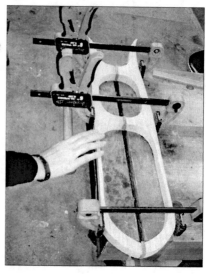

Cutting the Joint Pieces

From a different colored wood, cut three 1/4" thick by 1" by 2-3" pieces that you will sandwich glue into the three joints of the frame. If you are using light colored oak for your frame, you might use a dark walnut wood for the joints. These joints are very important so do not use a resiny wood as the glue will not hold well if too much natural resins are in the wood.

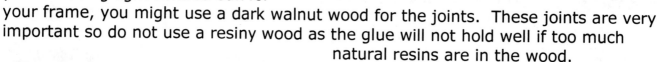

You could also build up a ply piece or purfling built up from many wood colors to add more ornamentation to sandwich into your three glue joints. Make sure the fit is very tight as these three joints hold the instrument together.

Gluing the Frame

Put sufficient glue on all of the glue joints on the frame and on both sides of the pieces of wood you will be gluing into the

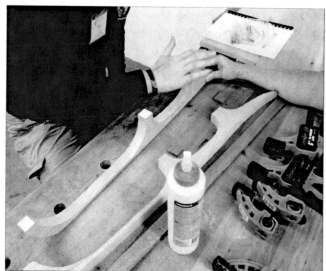

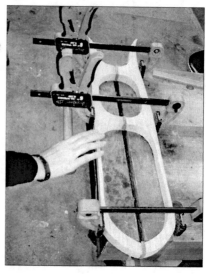

frame joints. On a flat surface with paper down, press the frame together with the small wood pieces in the joints. Clamp one of the joints (middle joint best) and then go to the next joint. I use small light 8" bar clamps for gluing the frame together.

Make sure the 1/4" wood joint pieces protrude slightly above the glue joint surface on both sides so they can be sanded down later to be made perfectly flat with the rest of the harp frame.

Clamping the bottom is the most difficult since it does not have a parallel surface to clamp easily. Some good heavy duty masking tape can be use to hold the bottom joint together as it dries.

Cleaning and Shaping

After the glue on the frame has hardened which is normally overnight left in a warm dry space, the clamps can be taken off. It is now time to clean up the joints by sanding or hand planing to assure the two pieces make a symmetrical shape of the lyre.

The inside of the hand hole for getting to the strings from the back can be sanded with a small drum sander or shaped by using a wood rasp, then finer wood file and then hand sanded. All of the external sides of the harp can be sanded now as a single piece and held up in the air to visually see the symmetrical shape of the lyre being formed.

The joints need to be sanded down so they are flush with no rises in the joint. The wood laminated in the joint also flat so the top and back may fit with no air or light seen between the joint from any view.

Final Form Sanding

At this stage, it is beginning to look like the final form of the lyre. You have completed the most difficult part of making the harp other than the final sanding that can be time consuming but easy.

Make sure you hold the harp up to the sky or a light wall to compare the evenness of both sides of the form as being symmetrical. What you accept now for the form is what is will be from now on. Take a little time and use the belt sander in the sides of the frame to get it into a very pleasant shape. Be sure to not sand off more than 3/16" width for the remaining width of the sides so you retain a solid surface for gluing on the top and back.

8. Top & Back

Preparing the Top and Back

It is here that the instrument needs most of its tuning for the top and the back before it is put together. The sound hole is very small - much smaller than a guitar sound hole and very difficult to get into to modify the instrument after it has been glued together. So it is best to do all that can be done before it is put together.

We already discussed the theory behind the tuning of the top and back. There are no inner braces on this instrument since the lower floating bridge provides all of the needed bracing. What we do need to do is to tune the top and the back so when they are glued onto the lyre frame, they provide for ultimate resonance.

The tone wood of the lyre should be planed and sanded to the right thickness which is about 1/8". Since you will be sanding it more later, it will become thinner to about 3/32" to 1/8" as it is tuned to become the top and the back of the lyre.

Cutting Out Top and Back

The next step is to place the top and back on the frame of the instrument and to mark the edges lightly with a pencil so you know what size to cut the top and the back. I would write 'top' on one piece and 'back' on the other on the inside so they do not get mixed up. I would also write 'top' and 'back' on the center of the frame so the frame

does not get glued upside down.

Now cut out both the top and the back about 1/4" outside the line with a bow saw, coping saw, band saw or Sabre saw. If you have a fine bladed jigsaw, this also works fine. I would also cut the angle, round off and sand the sound wood on the top and back areas where it meets with the arms of the lyre.

Tuning the Top

Now take the top and hold it vertical between your thumb and a finger near the top edge. Tap the sound board about in the middle and listen for the tone. If you have a piano or other instrument, you can determine the note of the tone you are hearing. Since the tone will go up about a 5th higher when it is in the instrument, we want to tune it a 5th lower. We want the top to sound with the note of D which is a 4th above A. Taking the note of D and transposing a 5th lower we land on the note of G#. By doing this, you will have designed the box to the note of A. Keep working by sanding the top until is rings with the note of G#. You may leave it a little thicker in the center while making it a little thinner around the edges if mass is needed. This will give you more adjustment room to get to the note you want.

As you will remember from the theory section, we want the instrument to resonate with all of the notes played and we have decided that the following notes for the three tunable parts of the instrument is best for our purposes.

I:	A = A, C# and E	Sound Box
IV:	D = D, F# and A	Top Soundboard
V:	E = E, G# and B	Back Soundboard

Since the top and back will raise about a fifth when glued, we drop the tones a 5th to be close to our resonating tones. For the back and top we tune to:

Top: <u>Tape Tone for G#</u> which is a 5th below the tone of D.

Back: <u>Tap Tone for A</u> which is a 5th below the tone of E.

You may also want to cut the sound hole about 2" wide prior to gluing on the top unless you have a drill press 2" hole boring saw such as used for cutting in door knobs through doors.

Gluing on the Top

Now that the top is rough tuned, you can glue on the top. 2" spring clamps work the easiest but strong masking tape also works well. The art of gluing is to place just enough glue in the joint that a little squeezes out evenly along the full length of the joint without it flowing down the sides. This assures the glue is well distributed and makes it easy for cleanup.

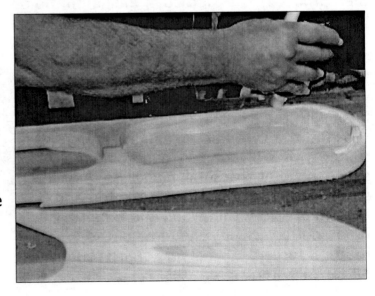

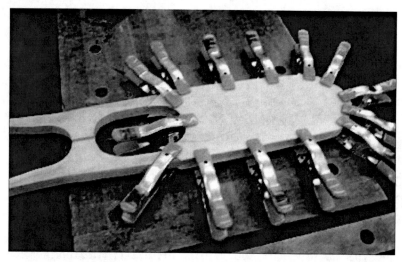

If you do get glue on the sides, you must quickly clean it off with a damp rag. If you don't, the glue will soak into the wood and not let the finish penetrate in causing a glue discoloration on your instrument. Be sure to align the bottom and top frame glue joints with the center of the soundboard.

Then clamp the top with a 2" spring clamp and followed by the bottom so it does not move. You can now clamp the rest of the sides about every 2-3 inches apart around its complete perimeter. Look carefully to assure there are no gaps in the glue joint. Set the frame and just glued on top aside in a warm dry place to dry overnight.

Tuning the Back

You will do the same process for the back except we want the final note to be a 5th above the box resonance which is the note of E. For this we tune the back a 5th lower to get E to the note of A. The back will be a little thicker and thus stiffer than the top if they are cut from the same wood. Again, you can leave more wood in the center of the back and lessor on the edges so the tone wood is able to vibrate more easily in resonance to the played strings while keeping needed mass for the tuning to E.

Gluing on the Back

Before gluing on the back, you need to decide if you plan to add an internal electric pickup to the instrument. If you do, go to chapter 9 and do this first. If not then proceed. The method of gluing on the back is the same process as gluing on the front.

Trimming the Sides

Once the lyre is glued together, you will need to trim the top and bottom flush with the sides of the frame. You can trim the Lyre flat or rounded by a router with 3/8" quarter round bit, small spokeshave or the small plane. Be careful to go very slow since the top and bottom are very thin wood and tend to break out (crack) by the force of the router if forced. Use a very sharp router bit for this step.

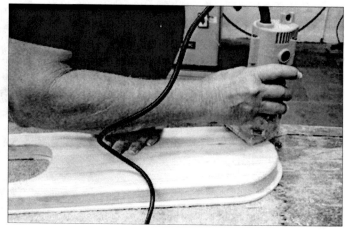

Fine Tuning Top and Back

When you tap tone the glued together, trimmed and sanded lyre, you will hear more than one resonate tone. You may need to put your ear close to the top and tap it to hear its tone. Hoping the pitch is a little higher than D, you can sand down the top a little more around the sides of the top where it connects to the frame to lower the pitch to D.

If it is lower than D and you need if higher, there is not much you can do about it except glue in some pieces of wood inside to increase the mass to make the tap tone pitch higher. This can be done without much loss in volume but should be dine with the same wood as the top and back using longer thin pieces of wood and glued very tight to the inside of the top or back near the resonate nodes or the bridge area.

Do the same for the back except it should be a tone of 'E'. Once the top and back are in tune you can then tune the sound box.

Cutting Sound Hole

The tuning of the sound box is largely through changing the size of the sound hole. First you have to cut the sound hole. A 2" to 2 1/2" hole saw in a drill press is best. If you cut the hole after it is all glued together, make sure you take out the pilot bit from the hole saw. Make sure the hole is centered. I usually center the hole 4" from the edge to the top and then center measuring from side to side.

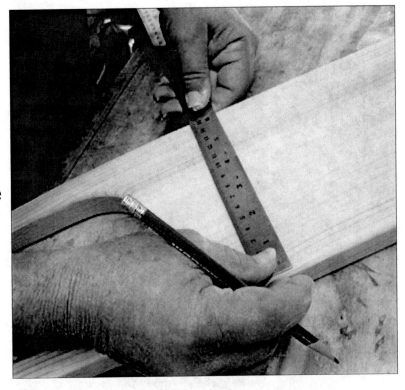

The box tuning cannot be done until the instrument is all glued together and the hole drilled. When the finish is put on, it will also add more mass to the instrument tone wood and again cause it to become a little stiffer and perhaps go a little higher in pitch.

Some instrument makers advocate using a very light weight finish such as shellac to not make the instrument heavier resulting in a change of tuning.

Tuning the Sound Box

Once the hole is drilled and the sides of the hole are sanded by hand to a round smooth edge, you may now tune the box. Just hum into the hole up and down in scales of pitch like a siren and listen until the instrument starts vibrating.

The pitch where it does start vibrating the loudest is usually the box resonance. You can again go to a piano or other instrument and check the pitch of the note until it vibrates the loudest wanting the tone of A for the sound box.

If the box resonance is higher than what you want, you can remove some of the wood around the sound hole in making it a little larger. This will lower the box tone. The picture here is using a forester bit that requires a drill press.

Once you have achieved the tuning of the top, back and box, you are ready to move on to finishing your lyre.

Test of Overall Tone

If you have tuned your instrument correctly, all of the notes in the Major scale of A to A, B and C# will have a strong resonance without any tone being muffled or weak. This is the test of a good instrument with full bodied base tones and bright treble tones.

9. Finishing

The choice of finish is critical to getting the best tone resonance from your instrument. I made one harp that a lady sent back to me after destroying it with her fingernails and said it did not have any finish on it. She explained to me it not having finish is why her fingernails were gouging into the soundboard. The fact is, it had 7 coats of hand rubbed satin urethane varnish and was well resistant to the conditions found in 'normal' use.

Key to a Good Finish

The most important key to a good finish is to sand the wood down and then buff the wood until is glows before any finish is applied. I will say this again, "Sand and buff the wood to a nice glow with 0000 steel wool before applying any finish." The finish will enhance and protect what is already there. If there are sanding marks left in your wood, the finish will nicely magnify these defects.

Also any glue residue needs to be scraped and sanded off - this also means the glue that soaked deep into the wood. To get this out of the wood, you will need to be sanded down to the raw wood or in some cases a solvent may be used. However, solvents may stain the wood and this would not be wanted. Always test on a scrap piece of wood before applying any untested solution to your prized instrument.

Too Much Finish

The fact is, if you put enough plastic on your instrument to be able to use it to go ice sledding down the mountain, it will not be a good sounding instrument. You can pick up any old quality instrument out of Europe and can press it with a fingernail and make a mark. <u>Don't ever try this – you may get imprisoned or shot!</u> The classical era luthiers commonly used shellac which comes from the dissolved bodies of bugs and is very light in weight. They would then mix a few secret ingredients into their shellac and then hand rub this warmed up finish into the instrument with many coats and sand / buff between each coat.

Spraying

If you are going to spray a finish on your instrument, use shellac, lacquer or one of the light spray plastics. Spray as thin a coat as possible and sand very lightly not going through the finish with fine paper between each coat. Just be sure not to build up the coats too thick as this will change the weight and tone of your instrument.

This is also true if foolishly refinishing a Stradivarius violin. By so doing, they never sound the same and many a beautiful instrument has been ruined by a well meaning Luthier who promised it would be as good as new after he or she was done with it. I have never heard of this occurring – an instrument being as good as new after refinishing almost never happens. It might occur if a very thick coat of plastic was removed from a cheaply made instrument and a lighter coat was then applied but most good instruments have thin coats of finish carefully applied. Finish and the type of finish used and how it is applied and how much is applied are the variables that will always tend to change the tone of an instrument.

Hand Rubbed

I personally prefer hand rubbed finishes. Tung oil and linseed oil are historic and have been used by some but I find these very long in drying in some climates and soak into the wood and make it very heavy. Shellac is still available as flakes and is normally dissolved in alcohol to provide a built-up hand rubbed finish. Manufacturers like Formbys and now big name brands provide a light hand rubbed urethane or lacquer finish that is easy to apply, fast drying with good results and is available in most home repair stores. Having buffed your wood to a dull shine will reduce the amount of finish that is absorbed into the wood and keep your instrument light in weight and more resonate.

Whatever finish you decide to use, be patient and take your time to give it the best surface possible with the least amount of finish. In so doing, you will have years of enjoyable use of your instrument as long as you keep it away from people with long aggressive fingernails who are prone to unknowingly attack your prized lyre without mercy and then complain about it not having any finish on it.

The soundboard above was made from western red cedar fencing that was thoroughly dried and then planned down to about 3/16" thickness by 5 1/2" in width. The symbol was wood burned into the lyre before the strings were put on.

10. *Hardware*

Checklist

Hardware for the lyre includes the 10 tuning pins, brads for attaching the strings at the base of the lyre and a small 1/16" rod used atop the lower bridge. The tuning pins are tuned with a tuning wrench so a Zither type tuning wrench is needed as well. To hold the strings at the bottom of the lyre, there are tie pins which are bright 3/4" long brads about 1/16" wide with large heads. Also there will be 10 monofiliment nylon strings as the music strings for the lyre. You will need the following hardware if you are making your lyre.

- 10 tuning pins (used for autoharps and zithers).
- 1 tuning wrench.
- 10 tie pins or brads for the bottom of the lyre.
- 1 - 5" by 1/16" metal rod for the lower bridge.
- 1 – 5 1/2" Wooden bridge.
- 10 monofiliment nylon strings in three sizes.

Drilling the Holes for the Tuning Pins

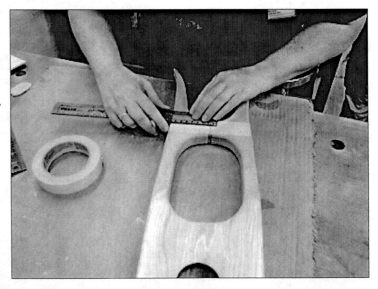

The challenge in drilling is to drill evenly spaced holes in the upper cross piece of the lyre slightly smaller than the size of the tuning pins. The more accurate you are in marking lining up these holes while also straight while drilling, the better the instrument will look.

The first thing to do is to set up a drill press to drill the holes. If you do not have a drill press, you can use an electric hand drill and make a jig so it will drill straight down every time. If you do not have an electric hand drill, you can use a hand powered drill but this is very challenging to get the holes evenly spaced and straight down at 90 degrees to the wood since your cranking of the hand drill gear is constantly moving the vertical alignment of the drill.

Before you drill the holes, set the center of the holes at exactly 10 mm apart by marking with a light pencil on masking tape placed down over the wood. You can use the glue joint as your guide for centering in placing 5 holes to the left and 5 holes to the right all exactly 10 mm apart. Then come back and take an awl and press a starter hole into the wood so the bit will center itself over the mark.

I would place a collar around the bit so it stops at a set depth or a piece of masking tape around the bit so you can stop it before it goes through the wood. The wood thickness for the tuning pins is as little as 3/4" thick in some instruments so you want to stop the depth at about 5/8" or 1/8" before it goes through the wood. If you ever accidentally drill through and out the back, you can place a small ornamental 1/8" thick piece of nice wood in the back side over the full area where the tuning pins are located to hide your mistake.

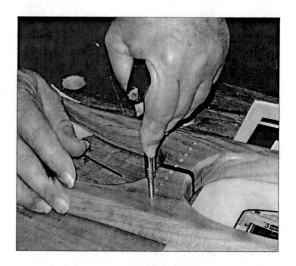

Drilling for Holes for the Tie Pins

There are 10 brads about 3/4" long and 1/16" in width with a large brad head that are used for the tie pins at the base of the lyre. This is not a straight line of holes like the tuning pins at the top but an arch so you have to first tape along the

bottom edge or corner of the lyre on up the side about 5 inches.

You will then find the joint at the bottom of the instrument and measure 5mm on the left side and 5mm on the right side about 3/8" up from the edge and mark it on the tape. You will then slide the metric ruler about 3/8" up and and make sure it aligns with the holes you just marked.

Then mark the next two holes also 3/8" from the edge. The edge is rounded so you measure in perpendicular to the edge. You do this again for the next two holes until you get all 10 holes marked.

Then you look at the symmetrical placement of the marks and and adjust the marks visually if needed. It is important to keep the distance of 10mm between your marks as the future location of the strings.

The next step is to use an awl and press a hole into the wood at the measured 'crossing' or + which is 3/8" in from the edge and up the sides in the shape of an arc for the the next set of holes going up around the sides of the lyre. If you are still confused, please look at the picture to the left for a visual of where the tie pin holes are to be placed on the lyre.

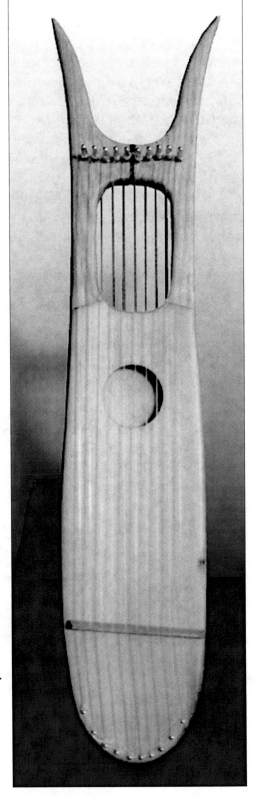

After having made the awl holes, you can now drill the holes for the tie pins with a bit slightly smaller than the width of the tie pins. You want these pins to go in snug and tight without any movement since they will be holding the tension all of your strings. The tie pins can be seated with a small chasing hammer being sure the back of the lyre is flatly placed on a solid non-moving surface such as a work bench.

You may put a cloth under the back of the lyre to keep the surface from making marks in the instrument. Be very careful to not miss the tie pin and hit the instrument with the hammer or it will leave a very nasty dent.

Making the Bridge

The bridge for the lyre spans completely across the instrument and is the only cross structural piece for the instrument. It is what conveys the sound of the strings to the top soundboard that then resonates the rest of the lyre. The bridge should be about 5" long and 1/2" high and about 1/4" at its base tapering to 3/32" at its top. On the top you will carve a grove the length of the bridge as a saddle for the 1/16" brass rod. The easiest way to do this is to use a small jewelers round file and your fingers as a guide and run the file back of forth parallel at the center of the bridge until is has a small groove that fits the rod.

Once the bridge is made and a saddle for the rod is carved, the rod itself will need very slight grooves perpendicular to the rod every 10mm to accept the strings going over the rod. A small jewelers triangular file or very small round file is usually best for this.

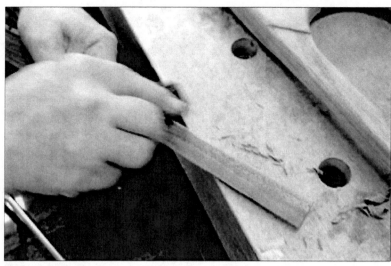

Find the center of the rod and measure out 5mm in each direction from the center for your first groves. Then place the rest of the grooves every 10mm with five on each side of center.

If the top is not exactly flat, you will need to shape the bottom of the bridge to the crowned shape of the top. The easiest way to do this is to tape a piece of 120 sand paper to the top and rub the bottom of the bridge back and forth in the direction of the length of the instrument until they fit perfectly.

You are now ready to put on the strings and tune the instrument in chapter 10.

11. Ornamentation

The ornamentation of the lyre is very impressive if done as a wood burning motif. The function of the wood burning tool is to create lines of the design and then shading from the lines to give it depth.

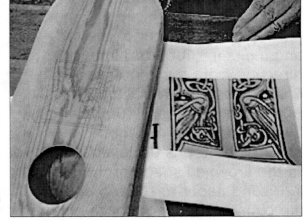

The easiest way to do this is to get some carbon paper and trace the design you have chosen on paper through the carbon paper to the bare wood of the instrument. I would tape off one end of the paper and carbon so it does not move while you lift the paper and carbon to see that the trace is dark enough on the the wood to then do the wood burning.

When wood burning, be careful not to hold the iron in one place too long. The top is only 1/8" thick and you could burn right on through the wood and leave a hole. I suggest you do a couple of designs on scrape wood from the top and back before actually burning the design. Practice keeping the iron moving on the wood as it burns to get an even burn depth and darkness on the wood.

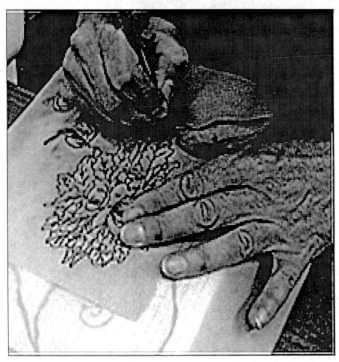

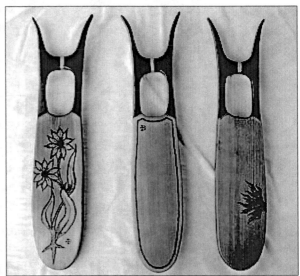

12. Electrics

The best time to install a pickup in a Mountain Lyre is before you glue the back on the instrument. There are some very inexpensive peizo elements that have been developed from simple peizo disks and work very well.

The best place to locate these pick-up devices is inside under where the bridge is located on the top of the soundboard. Many will install two elements – one on the bass side of the bridge and the other on the treble side of the bridge.

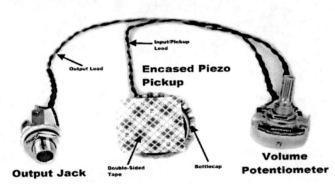

Encased Piezo Pickup

Input/Pickup Lead

Output Lead

Output Jack

Double-Sided Tape

Bottlecap

Volume Potentiometer

If you want a volume control, this can be added by soldering a potentiometer between the 1/4" RCA jack and the peizo element.

The best way to attach a pickup inside the instrument is to use 2-part epoxy resin so the contact is very secure.

It is advised to put the element within a thin block of wood that is of the same density as the soundboard or harder wood to reduce possible feed-back from the amp. This can be done by using a wide flange or forester bit slightly larger than the width of the element and embedding it into the wood block so it is the wood that is glued underneath the soundboard and not the element itself. This can also be glued with epoxy resin.

Another consideration is to add a pre-amp inside the instrument if you are an electronics kind of person and can build this from the following schematic. It does need a 9VDC battery so you have to work out this issue. This approach would have to be done before you glue the back on the lyre since you would likely not be able to get all this through the sound hole.

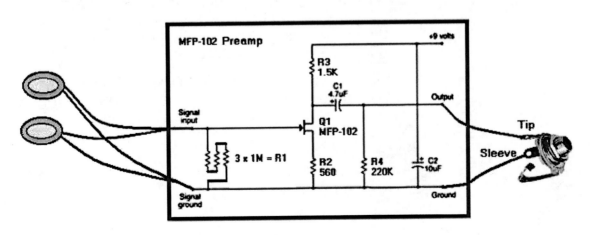

13. Tuning

The Set of Strings

You were given in the kit or with a finished instrument you would have 10 nylon monofiliment strings for the lyre. The lower three stings are the same size as are the next three strings and the last four strings are of the same size. Monofiliment strings provide the best tone when they are tensioned at about 80% of their breaking strength.

If you ever break a string, good quality fishing line works very well in a pinch. I suggest you buy the following weights in fishing line for the 10 strings of the lyre with string 1 being the lowest tonal string and string 10 being the highest tonal string.

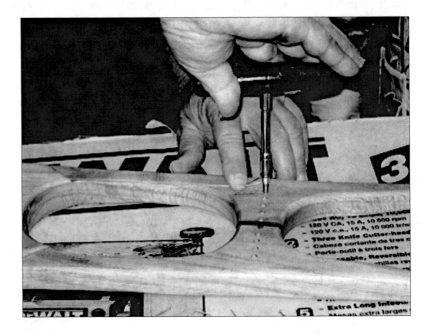

- 120 lb test
- 120 lb test
- 120 lb test
- 60 lb test
- 60 lb test
- 60 lb test
- 30 lb test
- 30 lb test
- 30 (20) lb test
10. 30 (20) lb test

From the chart of strings above, we can estimate the amount of pressure on the frame of the lyre when it is strung up to its proper playing pitch. Adding up all of the string weights above and then dividing by 0.8, we get about 500 pounds of pressure on the lyre or about ¼ tons of force.

This again shows how important our glue joints must be to hold the instrument together.

Tying Off the Strings

The tying of the nylon monofiliment strings onto the tie pins is perhaps the most challenging part of stringing and tuning the lyre. You simply tie the strings in a series of square knots on top of each other. For the low sounding first three stings, you should knot them about 5 times.

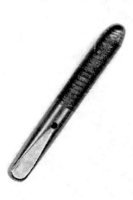

For the second three strings in the middle of the instrument, you should knot them about 7 times. For the lightest 4 strings you should knot them about 10 times. Also it is important that the top 4 strings be run through the tuning key string hole twice or they will start sliding and pull out when you are tuning them up to pitch.

Placing the Bridge

When you get the first low string strung, you can slide the bridge with the metal rod under this string and it will hold it all in place while you are putting the other strings on. The location of the bridge is as per the pictures you have seen earlier in this book.

Tuning

When all of the strings are on, increase the tension on them a little at a time across all 10 strings using a tuning key so the instrument has similar pressure on both sides. When you get the strings up to pitch, the strings and the knots around the tie pins will stretch for a few days until all the strings settle in. You can speed up this process a little by taking your thumb and fore finger and grasping a string in making an 'S' in the string to increase the tension on the string and ties making it stretch and settle in faster.

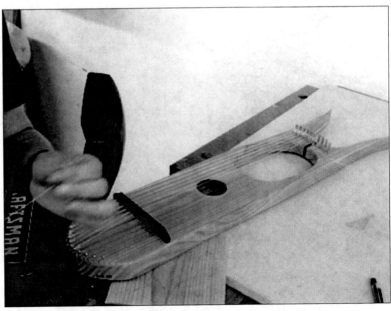

You will notice that the notes of F, C and G are all sharp in diatonic A Major but for pentatonic A Major where D and G# are not played, we have only 2 sharps in this scale. The scale for A Major is the following notes while not having the strings to play the notes found in parentheses.

A major scale

	A	B	C♯	D	E	F♯	G♯	A	B	C♯
	do	re	mi	fa	so	la	ti	do	re	mi
low	1	2	3	4	5	6	7	8	9	10

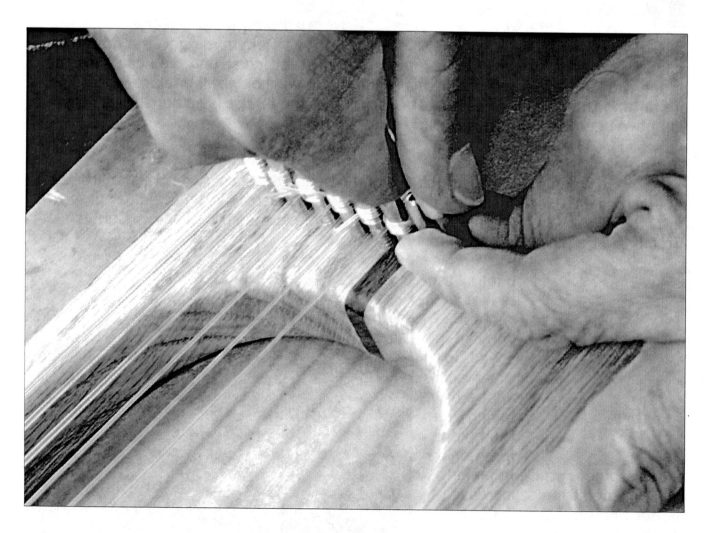

14. Playing

Holding

The way to hold the Mountain Lyre is normally done in a seated position while resting the bottom of the instrument on the middle of the top of the left thigh and then holding the top with the left hand. This frees up the right hand to play the notes. If playing through the hole with the left hand, the lyre can lean against the players left inside wrist while they use their left fingers to pluck the lower strings.

The lyre can also be played standing and although you can can hold it fully with the left hand and lean the instrument into your waist while standing or walking (marching), the addition of a guitar strap and strap 'buttons' screwed into the base and left horn of the instrument is recommended.

Single Note Playing

Playing one note at a time is the easiest way to play the lyre. Fingernails should be grown between 1/8" to 1/4" on your right hand thumb and fingers 1, 2 and 3. Seldom is the pinky finger used in playing the lyre. It is best to assign the fingers to play a set of strings where the same finger usually plays the same string all the time. Some have taken choral music and assigned each person with a lyre to play one voice each as a 2, 3 or 4 part harmony with the music being transposed into the range of the instrument. The easiest music for transposing is 2 to 4 part alto, soprano or tenor pentatonic music. Since the lyre can also be tuned to a diatonic scale from the normal pentatonic scale, the music will be limited to the key of A major or A minor in most cases.

Chording

To chord the lyre is by using your three fingers and thumb to pluck 2, 3 or 4 strings at the same time with the fingernails. Chording can also be an arpeggio strum. In the Pentatonic tuning, you can pluck any two notes spaced two or more strings apart to get a chord. Since the 4th and 7th tone is missing in the Pentatonic scale, you can pluck any two strings next to each other for a pleasant sounding interval. The strings that can be played adjacent to each other are C# - E, and F# - A.

Picking

The method of picking the lyre is predominately using the right hand with the option of playing some base notes through the hole with the left hand. The picking technique is easily adapted from classical guitar methods where fingernails are used to pluck the strings. Most any classical picking style can be used in finger picking with the thumb and three fingers.

Even flamenco style is possible if this is what you are trained to do on a guitar. The spacing of the lyre strings is 10mm and is based on the common spacing of many guitars. This allows a guitar player to adapt very easily to the lyre and move between the two instruments without any 'finger spacing' readjustment traumas since there is little or no difference in the string spacing.

This is the class where most of the pictures of this book comes from. Most of these students never made anything of wood before. They are naturally holding the lyre-harp correctly for playing with the base leaning in the lap or left thigh and slightly tilted to the left or any direction it feels comfortable. The right hand plays the upper notes with the left hand using the fore finger to play through the back for some of the low notes. The harp can be held or stabilized with the thumb of the left hand so it does not move around.

All of them made these harps within a week period from rough milled parts. Only 2 or 3 of these students had been in a wood shop before. They used an early draft of this book and provided many suggestions to make this book better.

15. Transposing

Folk Songs

There are numerous songs written in the diatonic or pentatonic scale with many being well known Folk songs found in different cultures all around the world. The down side is that many of them are not written in the key of A and cannot be played on the lyre without being transposed from their current key to the key of A major.

Transposing Notes and Chords in Keys

If you find a song that is not in the key of A, then you will need to transpose the music to the key of A Major. An easy way to do this is to use the following charts. The following charts provide for transposing from key to key on a note by note basis.

The key signature (left) tells you what key it is in by counting the number of sharps or flats shown at the beginning of the staff. If there are three sharps in this signature, we know it is the key of A Major. The following chart shows the names of the notes and their placement of the Grand Staff and which keys of the piano play these notes.

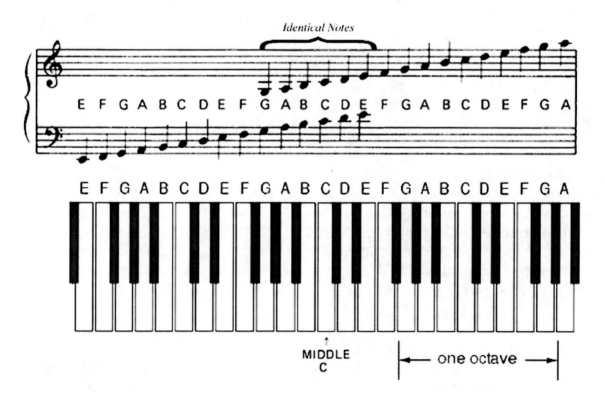

Below, we find the note names of the staff lines and the staff spaces. EGBDF are the notes for the lines of the Treble staff and can be remembered by the phrase, "Every Good Boy Does Fine." And for the spaces, we simply remember FACE. Both are read up from the bottom of the staff.

For transposing a simple melody line, you simply identify the key that it is written in and then find the note of music on the staff, know its letter name using the chart and then go across the chart below to the key of A Major and use that letter and note instead. It is easiest to use pre-printed music staff paper for transposing music for the lyre. When you have done this for all of the notes in the melody, you are then ready to play the music in the new key of A major.

As an example, when transposing the key of Db Major where you see 5 flats in the key signature, look to the left of the chart below and start transposing each note to A Major. The notes in parenthesis in the charts below are not found in the pentatonic scale of these keys but they are used in the diatonic keys.

Db: Old Key	Db	Eb	F	Gb	Ab	Bb	C
A: New Key	A	B	C#	D	E	F#	G#

Key \# or b	A 3 #	Bb 2 b	B 5 #	C none	Db 5 b	D 2 #	Eb 3 b	E 4 #	F 1 b	Gb 5 b	G 1 #	Ab 4 b
I	A	Bb	B	C	Db	D	Eb	E	F	Gb	G	Ab
ii	B	C	C#	D	Eb	E	F	F#	G	Ab	A	Bb
iii	C#	D	D#	E	F	F#	F	G#	A	Bb	B	C
IV	D	Eb	E	F	Gb	G	Ab	A	Bb	B	C	Db
V	E	F	F#	G	Ab	A	Bb	B	C	Db	D	Eb
vi	F#	G	G#	A	Bb	B	C	C#	D	Eb	E	F
vii	G#	A	A#	B	C	C#	D	D#	E	F	F#	G

Minor Key Transposing

What if the song you want to transpose is in a minor key? This means that the minor vii of C# in the key of A Major is lowered ½ step and becomes a minor chord iii with the change of C# being lowered to C. A then becomes the tonic or beginning note of the new A minor scale by only changing one note in the scale. In re-tuning the lyre to play in the new A minor scale, you will have to tune down the two C# strings on your lyre to the note of C.

Chord Transposing

An easy way of transposing more complex chords if these are provided in the music you are transposing is to use a chord transposing chart. If you were playing in the key of C Major with the chords of C, F, G7 and Am, when you transpose to the key of A Major, it will now be the chords A, D, E7 and F#m.

TRANSPOSING CHART

KEY OF	KEY SIGNATURE																	
C	(treble clef)	C	F	G7	Am	Dm	A7	D7	E7	F7	C7	B7	Em	Fm	Gm	G	Bb	G+	C#°7
G	(1♯)	G	C	D7	Em	Am	E7	A7	B7	C7	G7	F#7	Bm	Cm	Dm	D	F	D+	G#°7
F	(1♭)	F	Bb	C7	Dm	Gm	D7	G7	A7	Bb7	F7	E7	Am	Bbm	Cm	C	Eb	C+	F#°7
D	(2♯)	D	G	A7	Bm	Em	B7	E7	F#7	G7	D7	C#7	F#m	Gm	Am	A	C	A+	(Eb°7) D#°7
Bb	(2♭)	Bb	Eb	F7	Gm	Cm	G7	C7	D7	Eb7	Bb7	A7	Dm	Ebm	Fm	F	Ab	F+	B°7
A	(3♯)	A	D	E7	F#m	Bm	F#7	B7	C#7	D7	A7	(Ab7) G#7	C#m	Dm	Em	E	G	E+	(Bb°7) A#°7
Eb	(3♭)	Eb	Ab	Bb7	Cm	Fm	C7	F7	G7	Ab7	Eb7	D7	Gm	Abm	Bbm	Bb	Db	Bb+	E°7
E	(4♯)	E	A	B7	C#m	F#m	C#7	F#7	(Ab7) G#7	A7	E7	(Eb7) D#7 (Abm) G#m	Am	Bm	B	D	B+	F°7
Ab	(4♭)	Ab	Db	Eb7	Fm	Bbm	F7	Bb7	C7	Db7	Ab7	G7	Cm	Dbm	Ebm	Eb	Gb	Eb+	A°7
B	(5♯)	B	E	F#7	(Abm) G#m	C#m	(Ab7) G#7	C#7	(Eb7) D#7	E7	B7	(Bb7) A#7 (Ebm) D#m	Em	F#m	F#	A	F#+	C°7
Db-C#	(5♭/7♯)	C# Db	F# Gb	G#7 Ab7	A#m Bbm	D#m Ebm	A#7 Bb7	D#7 Eb7	E#7 F7	F#7 Gb7	C#7 Db7	B#7 C7	E#m Fm	F#m Gbm	G#m Abm	G# Ab	B Cb	G#+ Ab+	D°7
F#-Gb	(6♯/6♭)	F# Gb	B Cb	C#7 Db7	D#m Ebm	G#m Abm	D#7 Eb7	G#7 Ab7	A#7 Bb7	B7 Cb7	F#7 Gb7	E#7 F7	A#m Bbm	Bm Cbm	D#m D#m	F#	E Fb	C#+ Db+	G°7

Chart from SteelGuitarForum.com

Transposing Practice

There are many pentatonic folk songs provided in the next section of this book that you will need to transpose before you can play them on the lyre. Since the lyre is normally played in A major or A minor diatonic or pentatonic keys, transposing will become a common process to ready many new songs you will want to play on the lyre.

16. Songs

Alabama Gal

American Folk song

1.Come through in a hur - ry, come through in a hur - ry,

come through in a hur - ry, A - la - ba - ma Gal!

2. I don't know how, how,
I don't know how, how,
I don't know how, how,
Alabama Gal!

3. I'll show you how, how,

4. Ain't I rock candy?

Buck-eyed Jim

Appalachian folk song

1. Way down yon-der, a - bove the sky, a blue-bird lived in a jay-bird's eye.___

Refrain

Buck-eyed Jim, you can't go. Go weave and spin, you can't go. Buck-eyed, buck-eyed Jim.

2. Way up yonder above the moon,
   A bluejay nests in a silver spoon. *Refrain*

3. Way down yonder on a hollow log,
   A red bird danced with a green bullfrog. *Refrain*

Swing Low Sweet Chariot

CAMPTOWN RACES

STEPHEN FOSTER

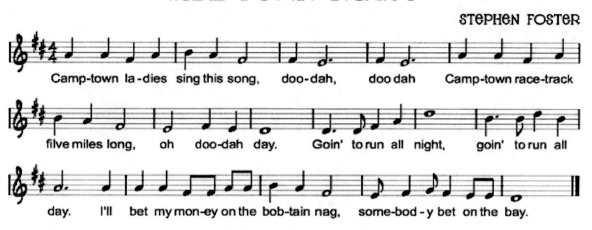

Camp-town la-dies sing this song, doo-dah, doo dah Camp-town race-track

filve miles long, oh doo-dah day. Goin' to run all night, goin' to run all

day. I'll bet my mon-ey on the bob-tain nag, some-bod-y bet on the bay.

This Train

African American Spiritual

This train is bound for glo - ry this train.___

this train is bound for glo - ry this train,___

this train is bound for glo - ry if you ride it you must be ho - ly

this train is bound for glo - ry this train.

Abbot David Michael,

Bought Me a Cat

Folk song

3. duck... quack, quack
4. goose... hissy, hissy
5. pig... oink, oink
6. sheep... baa, baa
7. hog... griffy, griffy
8. cow... moo, moo
9. horse... neigh, neigh
10. dog... bow-wow, bow-wow

All Night, All Day

African American Spiritual

All night, all day. Ang-els watch ing ov-er me, my Lord.

All night, all day. Ang-els watch ing ov-er me.

When I lay me down to sleep. Ang-els watch ing ov-er me, my Lord.

Pray the Lord my soul to keep. Ang-els watch ing ov-er me.

Old Dan Tucker

Traditional Folk Song

1.Old Dan Tuck - er was a might - y man, Washed his face in a fry - ing pan.
2.Old Dan Tuck - er came to town, Rid - ing a billy goat, leading a hound.
3.Old Dan Tuck - er came to town, swingin' the la - dies 'round and round.

Combed his hair with a wa - gon wheel, Had a tooth - ache in his heel, so
Hound dog barked and the billy goat jumped. Dan fell off and landed on.a. stump,
Circle to.the right, circle to the left, Swing the girl you love the best.

Get out the way, Old Dan Tuck - er, you're too late to get your sup - per,

Sup - per's o - ver and din - ner's cook - in',

Old Dan Tuck - er stands there look - in'.

Jubilee

Folk song

Sakura

Japanese folk song

Sa - ku - ra, Sa - ku - ra, Ya - yo - i - no - so - ra - wa.

Mi - wa - ta - su - ka - gi - ri - ka - su - mi - ka - ku - mo - ka.

Ni - o - i - zo, i - zu - ru. I - za - ya. I - za - ya. Mi - ni - yu - kan.

17. Composing

Rules of Composition

In the study of classical music that is the root of all modern music, rules emerge that were held to very rigidly for the composition of any style of music during the 17th and 18th centuries. It sounds classical only because it follows the rules of classical music with the various composers such as Beethoven, Mozart, Haydn and Salieri and others who help solidify these rules when they composed their music. The rules helped them decide the acceptable sequence of notes, the acceptable harmony structures resulting in the sequence of chords that were formed with these harmonies artistically erupting into excitement and then resolve with the ending of the music.

Our pallet for composing is limited to only using the following 10 notes which are two octaves in the pentatonic scale of A Major.

A major scale

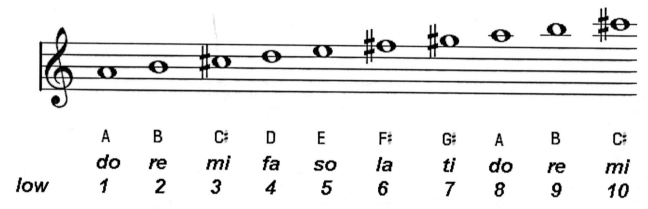

	A	B	C♯	D	E	F♯	G♯	A	B	C♯
	do	re	mi	fa	so	la	ti	do	re	mi
low	1	2	3	4	5	6	7	8	9	10

Composing in Diatonic A Major

The art of composing in scale of A Major is very easy. Anyone can do this with the adoption of an ancient method called 'Makam' invented by the Hebrews. It consists of a series of short musical phrases that are commonly found in all music that can be intuitively placed together in a sequence to create a new song by following a few simple musical rules. You do not have to know these rules in this book because they are provided in the composition cards where making a 'rule' mistake is near full proof.

Here are some other terms you should know while composing your new music.

- **Phrase (Makam):** 2-5 notes in sequence as found on the cards provided.
- **Sentence:** Many phrases are put together to complete a line of music. Example: "Oh home on the range, where the deer and the antelope play."

- **Verse:** 2 to 4 sentences together usually on a single theme that makes up a completed section of the music.
- **Chorus:** A varied set of 2-4 sentences that contrasts the verses musically.
- **Bridge:** This is yet another melody that is usually more radical and is used sparingly in a song to add variety between groups of verses and chorus. This can be a key change, the embellishment of a musical interlude or other musical sentence.
- **Song:** The completed song that develops with musical excitement and then normally resolves to a place of peace or repose in the end.

Sequencing the Composition Cards

In this chapter, you will find a series of staff cards that you can photocopy and then cut out as your deck of music composition cards for writing original music. You can thro9ugh experimentation decide which of the are best suited for in a musical sentence. If they are best as the opening of a song, then you can put an 'S' for Start on the card. If they work well anywhere in the middle of the song, they you can put a 'M' for Middle. If the phrases are good for a chorus sentence or4 harmony works, you can put a 'C' on the card for Chorus'. If they are good for a high harmony or special section like a descant somewhere in the song to add variety to the music, you can write a 'B' for bridge on the card. If they are good to use as the ending of a song with the feeling or completion and resolve, they should have a 'E' written on the card for good Ending.

Some of the phrase cards can be placed in many different places in the song so they may have 2 up to all 5 location descriptors.

1. **S (Start):** used as the first card for the start of the song.
2. **M (Middle):** may be used most anywhere in the middle of the song.
3. **C (Chorus):** may be used as a descant or chorus.
4. **B (Bridge):** Use to add musical variety and contrast to music. It is often found between a set of verses and the chorus.
5. **E (Ending):** Good for the end of a sing to bring a feeling of resolve to the music.

Experimenting with Melody

The best way to compose is to lay out about 5 cards in the recommended descriptor sequence and then play the tune on the lyre. If the sequence of intervals sounds good, you are ready to give time values to the notes and write your vocal verses. If you think it lacks something musically, you can swap around the cards, take away cards or add more cards to modify the melody and then try playing it again.

Giving Time Values to Notes

You will notice that the notes are all whole notes on the cards. This does not mean you have to keep it as such but you should play through the song and decide if some of these notes should be Eighth, Quarter or Half notes.

This means that in 4/4 time with 4 counts or beats in a measure, the eighth note will have ½ beat, the quarter note will have one beat and the half note will have 2 beats. You might also want to add rests here and there at the end of a musical sentence.

Note Values

Name	Symbol	Value	Rest
Breve	‖o‖	o + o	⊏⊐
Whole Note	o	o + o	▬
Half Note	♩	♩ + ♩	▬
Quarter Note	♩	♪ + ♪	𝄽
Eighth Note	♪	♪ + ♪	𝄾
Sixteenth Note	♬	♬ + ♬	𝄿
Thirty-second Note	♬	♬ + ♬	𝅀

"Common Time"

Four beats per measure

Quarter note gets the beat

"Cut Time"

Two beats per measure

Half note gets the beat

"Waltz Time"

Three beats per measure

Quarter note gets the beat

"6/8 Time"

Six beats per measure

Eighth note gets the beat

Measure Time Signature

You can decide to use a 2 beat measure, a 3 beat measure, a 4 beat measure or even a 6 beat measure when composing your original music. These are identified in music with a time signature. To the left you will notice a top number and a bottom number in the signature. The top number tells you how many beats per measure whereas the bottom number tells you what note gets one beat.

The division of the measures are represented by a vertical line in the measure called a bar. All music has so many beats per measure and you can decide what is best for your song. You can do this by playing through a sentence and count how many beats it has to the end of the musical sentence. You can ask yourself where is the natural emphasis in the beats in your musical sentence Does it occur naturally every 4th beat or every 3rd beat?

Eight measures per sentence is most common with each measure having 4 beats per measure with the quarter note getting one beat. You might start out with this for your first composed songs. This leaves room for experimentation when you get more comfortable with composing music in changing the length of the musical sentence and also the key signature to have alternately 2, 3 or 6 beats per measure.

Working the Cards

In the next chapter you will find numerous phrase composition cards and some blank cards where you can make your phrase melodies. The descriptors you put in are to help you order the cards but you are not bound to follow even your own rules. In some cases, you may use an ENDING phase at the beginning of a song and a BEGIN phrase at the end of the song. However, it is better to go along with what seems natural in the beginning of song writing until you have more experience.

18. Composition Cards

Photocopy this page and cut out to use cards.

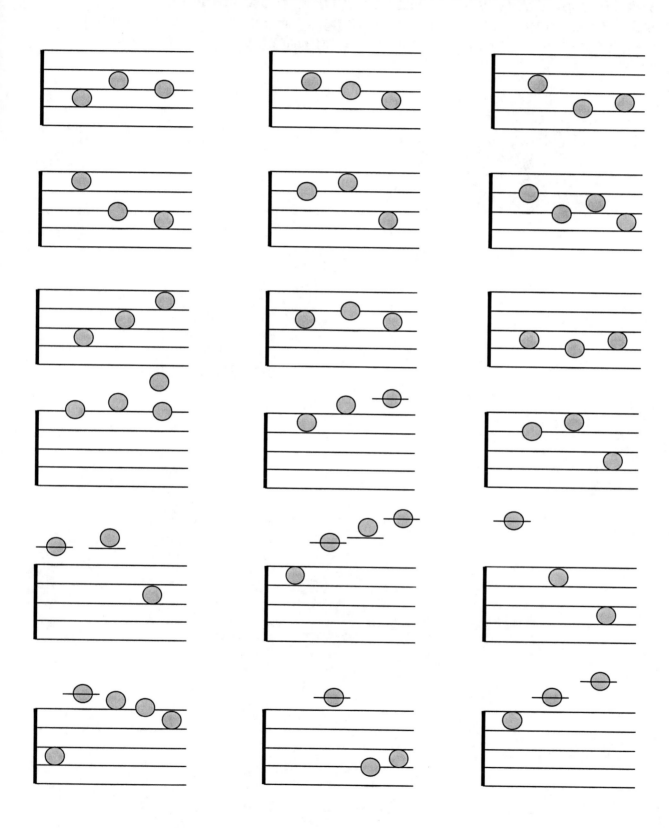

Extra Cards

Photocopy this page and cut out to make cards.

19. Harp Pattern

This pattern for the Lyre harp is provided to the right so you may create a template for making the frame of the harp. It will also give you the general dimensions of the back and front of the instrument and the bridge which is normally 1/4" shorter than the width of the instrument so it rests on the frame through the top wood.

It is best take piece of paper about 36" long (tape some together) so you can draw it out by placing the dimension marks on the paper and then free hand draw the curves. The sides are about 1/4" with a wider 1/2" along the bottom to hold the tension of the pins.

It is best to use the template and draw the two halves on paper to assure the match well and to see the overall form of the instrument. If you do not like the aesthetics of the form, modify the frame template until it looks good to the eye.

You can use a 4" piece of wood if your wood is longer than 36" by drawing one side then turning over the template and drawing the other so the glue joints are set into each other off-set. It is a little harder to cut out this way but is a good conservation of wood if you are using some very nice figured hardwood. If you take a 3" piece of 2" or thicker wood, you can cut down the center to get two 1" pieces of wood and have your frame book-match for the sides.

Have fun and know there is not absolute correct design. Feel free to experiment.

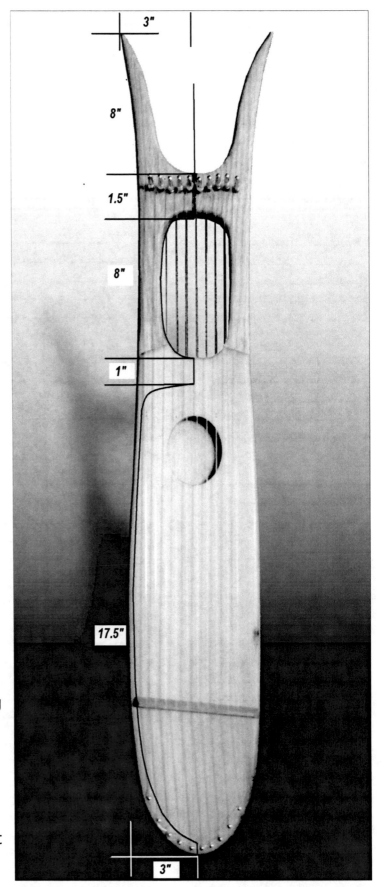

20. Kits & Bio

Battleharp.com

Want a harp kit or a completed harp? Battleharp.com is the place to get harp kits and hand-made finished instruments. You can even buy online using a charge card or PayPal account and have it shipped out in a few days. A tool kit of everything you would need to make harps is also in the works and will be available soon. Check on the battleharp.com web site periodically for the latest update of what we are offering at the very best prices.

http://battleharp.com

Bio of Abbot David Michael, ThD

Abbot David has been making instruments since 1975 when he apprenticed under George Gilmore, the favored student of Andre' Segovia. David has made hundreds of harps of various kinds including the only archaeologically correct Temple Kinnor of the bible period. Levites in Jerusalem purchased 6 of David's Temple harps to use when the Temple is rebuilt.

Abbot David holds a BA (High Honors) in Production in the Performing Arts with K-12 Teacher Certification in music to teach both primary and secondary education classes and K-12 certification in theater. He also holds a MEd in Educational Administration and a MS (with Distinction) in Information Systems. In addition, David earned a graduate certification in Historic Preservation, a DD in Ministry and a ThD in Anglo-Celtic Theology.

After many years teaching K-12 and college classes in Hawaii, Japan and Colorado, he is now a full-time author and has published 7 books on various subjects spanning such topics as the New World Order, aliens, career strategies, music theory, instrument making, composing musical operas and a handbook in the writing on Hebrew-Christian theology.

Today Abbot David lives at St. Michaels Abbey in the high mountains of Colorado at 10,000 foot elevation and raises llamas, sheep and has a mule. If you would like to contact him directly, he can be reached at **info@glentivar.org**.

Other Books by Abbot David Michael

http://glentivar.org

CPSIA information can be obtained at www.ICGtesting.com
Printed in the USA
LVOW09s1559170516

488668LV00013B/432/P